all of her healing

Alexandra Heather Foss

DEDICATION

For my son. My wish come true.

I love you, my little Oliver.
I'll love you forever and ever.

ACKNOWLEDGMENTS

The Acknowledgment sections of these books have been the most challenging part about them for me. I nearly didn't publish because I felt upset, and hurtful, for not being able to include everyone deserving of my thanks. But if I did, that would be these books in their entirety.

Every part of our daily lives is a result of a long chain of people. I bite a strawberry and think how once that was a seed, in soil someone tended, of all the people responsible for making that small piece of fruit accessible to me. The vitally important music in my life takes teams to create, produce, and distribute. Even the mother spider between the glass pane and screen in my bathroom window, who for years has made my days a little less lonely, I am grateful for.

The trees, a plate full of my mother's cooking, the vinyl records my son and I listen to in the morning, all of these are part of my healing journey. There is always someone we know, or meet, perhaps some author, or sunset, that beckons our gratitude, in any given moment. Without the sweet potato fries with feta and honey, from our local Greek restaurant, I might have stopped eating altogether after my heartbreak. And the characters and storyline of the television show *Hart of Dixie* have brought me comfort for years.

I emphasize and elaborate on the people I have usually because of the volume of experience, and the levels of intimacy and impact. I could list every song that has ever gotten me through a hard time or filled me with joy, but *The Phantom of the Opera* score I sing with my mother around the piano is special. Time has proven it more than the fun pop song that marks a season. Both matter, just differently.

Regardless of when or what I am writing, certain people are going to stand out. My son, father, mother, they are my rocks. The people who most stick. The people I most love. My mother has been with me, in one form or another, nearly every day of my life. My father brings me bags full of cough drops, or groceries, when I am too weak to get them myself, as does he make sure my car is well oiled, and running smoothly, when I can't. The hugs from my son daily boost my heart.

The people I value most are kind, they care, they accept difference, and they tend to listen and see with heart. I have a primary immunodeficiency, which means I am on antibiotics more than off most years, so I especially need everyone in my life, not just for emotional sustenance but survival. It is hard to be sick a lot. It can be scary. And exhausting. I am uncertain of time, how much there will be. So all the people who show up with their love are the reason I am even here to offer thanks.

I got through high school with assistance from Patsy Zendel, Don Fleming, and Linda Hamilton. They believed in my potential, and didn't give up on me. I largely think I made it to college with their help. There was Beverly, in the Spiral Circle Bookstore, my Rollins College teachers and experience, Elle, Mrs. Corbett, Walkabout, West Center Dance, Mary Acunzo, and Mr. Pettibone. Dr. Murray delivered my child, Hani saved my leg and life in Tahiti, Dr. Barney got me walking again, Anna Delude was there throughout my pregnancy, Dr. Pedersen is working to help me have my healthiest life, and Beth Felter is one of the most gentle and responsive doctors I know. Without the encouragement from Poets, I might have given up writing, and everyone who publishes my work has helped me to believe in myself and my words.

I asked my son a while back what he wanted to learn more about. He is an intelligent and curious boy, who will no doubt always be engaged in learning, but right now it is trees, and why Mama gets sick. I bought him books on each, and we have been studying them, learning the difference between maple leaves and seeds, and what a white blood cell is supposed to do. It makes me sad, that at only four, my son has been exposed to such serious topics as his mother's health, but as he is learning about illness, he is also learning about fortitude, and what it means to fight for life.

It takes courage to live. Courage to get up every day, to keep going in the face of uncertainty, to believe more in the good than anything bad that may happen, and that is true for all of us. Life isn't easy. Healing is hard. To keep our hearts open, to confront our shadow sides, to be honest and real, so we can integrate and mend, requires enormous courage, and personal strength.

The reason I keep going is because I love life. I love the mystery, the majesty, the galaxies in the eyes of everyone I have loved, the way my grandparents laughed, the sounds of the birds. I want to know what comes next, in the here and now, on this planet, in this form. Parts of my body don't work as they should, but my heart is almost invincible, as is my will to live.

Right now, we live in a world where disease is everywhere. Those of us who are immunocompromised are never certain about time, or safety, but for everyone, since this pandemic started, normal is gone. We all have been forced to adapt, at a rate that is uncomfortable, and scary.

What I have seen within this terrifying time, however, is a restored belief in magic. My neighborhood went from celebrating no holidays to all of them, so that now my son can go door to door on Halloween, and throughout the year, neighbors stop outside their homes, or on walks down the street, to say hello. We are spending more time with family, less time with less important distractions, and although there is the global heaviness of sadness, for everyone taken too soon, for those of us still here, there is renewed hope in the human capacity to adapt and persevere. I am proud to be part of a species that is so resilient.

I think it is also important that we show pride for and thank ourselves, in any list of gratitude. Which is a big adult step for me. When I was a girl, I said prayers at night. I don't practice a particular religion now, even though I was raised within one, but I do believe in a Divine force. I believe it isn't just us in this vast expanse of space, that there is more than only atoms and time. Because I believe, I prayed. I prayed for all the people I love, and the things, ending always with myself.

I love me the most, I would say.

Somewhere in the journey I lost that somewhat. I didn't stop loving myself, because no one would fight as hard as I have, to be here, did I not, but I did forget what it consciously means to have self-love. We never should forsake ourselves.

We are at least as important as the people we know, and we are the only ones who are there with and for us, every step.

Thanks is about telling those we cherish that we see them, as do we love them as they are. And so for everyone in my life I care about, then and now, as well as everyone yet to come, you are seen by me, and appreciated.

PREFACE

Much of what healing means to me I have already covered, at least in terms of gratitude. But when I started separating these poems into the three categories, I was surprised by this book, and it showed me something I hadn't realized.

Even when I went through all my posts in 2020, rereading them start to finish, over a short period of time, I read allofherworld as a story of pain, and love. I only saw it as a response to heartbreak, and a poem to someone I wish I had.

I knew I needed at least three books, when I learned that most poetry books are supposed to only include 100 poems or so (and even still these books have many more than that), but the third category was a bit of a mystery.

I chose healing, because I realized that is what my writing account ultimately has been. Making art of my feelings has been my primary means for healing. Yes, there are people, significant to my journey. No, I wouldn't be here without them. But it is the almost daily practice I have, of composing poems, and sharing them on allofherworld, and now also photographs, shared through withlovefromcapecod, that has helped me feel better inside, individual from any one person, or thing.

Healing is complicated. It isn't a linear process or a finite state of being. We are constantly revisiting and revising who we are and what we want, in the context of our ever-evolving life experiences, and emotions.

That doesn't mean we can't have a solid core. I do, which is why some of my favorite songs are the same now as they were thirty years ago, and why I have only been in love twice. There are things that never change. But so much about our understanding of self and other does.

My favorite poems are spread out between all three of these books. *all of her pain* is still how this started. *all of her love* is mostly all a love poem. But *all of her healing* is the fullest book. The one in a sense I see myself most in, inside nearly every poem.

It begins with the letter I wrote to my child, less than a week before he was conceived, the prayer for him really, which even at that time illustrated a powerful and catalyzing hope within me. It is filled with words that illuminate the healing journey. And it finishes with a short fictional story I wrote years ago, about a lonely table, searching for a home. A story, that although different from everything else in these books, I included, because rereading it now, I see in essence the story of myself.

Despite how broken loss left me, how desperately I wish every day for romantic love as I would want it, it is healing that most defines this last set of years for me.

That is not something I knew. I almost had to break these up to see how far I have come. To see that, although I am most focused on other, in my consciousness, it is myself that I am daily tending. allofherworld. All of *her* world. A play on my son Oliver's name, but for who I am, who I have been, who I am becoming.

I am not the same woman I was before. Which makes me think none of us who have gone through or are going through trauma of any kind, are. A lot happens under the surface of our understanding. We are becoming as we are wanting, whatever it is that we do.

What I hope you will read in these pages, what I hope this book will leave you with by the end, is faith. Faith that healing can happen, faith that you are strong, faith that regardless of anything that has or has not been, and will or will not be, you will go on. You will be healthier. Maybe not the same, maybe not resolved, or completely content, maybe always in process of some kind, but healthier for having continued the journey. Piecing together your pieces as best you can.

And if I can, however far I still have to go, you can. As long as you believe in yourself, and all the things that make you and your precious heart special.

Do not lose hope.

Do not give up.

You owe it to yourself to be as healthy as is possible, for as long as life gives you.

As do I.

Healing requires infinite bravery.

Dearest Child,

  I am your mother. I am writing to you like this because I am
afraid, terrified actually, that we may never meet. In the arms of
heartbreak, at an advanced age where childbearing is risky,
circumstance may keep us apart. If that is so, if I am unable to
give birth to you, I hope at least that Time and Space will concede
to grant these words passage. It is paramount you know you are
not alone. And that you are loved.

  I imagine you in different ways. Not so much with flaxen hair
or scarlet, with eyes brown like a plucked chestnut, or dewy as
morning grass, not with skin caramel, or pale as the moon, your
form for me is not fixed by shape or hue. Rather, you are light,
you are energy, the laughter that has never known pain, the
synthesis of every pure and beautiful moment, a symphony of
sound and movement. In the fabric that spreads out between here
and there, you are an unbreakable thread. You could be in etheric
perpetual motion in the center of a nebula, perhaps you are in the
bosom of an angel, wherever you are, however you are, whether
you are ugly or beautiful, good or bad, sick or healthy, you are
mine, and always will I love you. That fact, you can trust, as holy.

  This earthly life is hard, at times impossible, in fact often I have
wanted to give up. To tell you otherwise, to lure you to my womb
with false promises, would be a siren call. You deserve better.
You deserve real. So I will tell it to you like it is, or has been for
me, and hope only that my raw truth will entice you more than a
gilded lie.

  Earth is a planet of complex contradictions. Skin is as varied as
dreams, there are infinite ways matter takes form. A breath of
wind, a crescent lullaby, a swirling tornado, a snake rattling inside
a nest of palm fronds, an unappreciated trolley conductor hungry
for a hug, you might initially be confused by all the voices, colors,
and shapes. Our world is loud, it is violent, it is chaotic. We are
given five senses but often these get muddled and overwhelmed,
especially when peddlers try to sway us away from center. Never

let your inner compass be recalibrated from who you are.

Respect life but also fear it. Change is unavoidable, so never get too comfortable, and yet make sure to build a family, and a strong home, one internal, and one external, because a foundation well-built will give you at least some security, especially when life gets sick or stormy. You will lose, sometimes more than you gain. The use of your legs, hope, loved ones. Your heart will be crushed and it will feel like you cannot go on. It is then that you must. Rely on earthly angels to guide you and never let disappointment disenchant you away from living.

Whether arrogant, vicious, or greedy, no part of existence is unworthy. A mosquito, an amoeba, a vine, a homo-sapien, everything is important and vitally connected. The latter is the only group I can speak of with any degree of empirical awareness. Homo-sapiens have many strengths and many vices, we are a species like Janus, whole onto ourselves, but also divided. Simultaneously we face opposite directions, between past and future, sin and love, eternally we are torn between what is left and what is right. Inside the human skin is a veritable emotional playground where hate, loathing, gratification, ecstasy, honor, justice, prudence, virtue, and deceit indiscriminately comingle. For this reason, life can be confusing and it can be challenging to find contentment.

Life will touch you the right way but also the wrong way. I am so sorry about that. Learn when to say yes and when to say no, and only say either if you really mean them. Never be afraid to speak your truth. Or make mistakes. The only way to guarantee failure is to never try. Your personal identity and experience are as valuable as any other, even mine. Stay brave and remember you are sacred and that you deserve the best. I will try to give it to you, but you must also believe in yourself and your emotional, mental, and spiritual capacity. Use your gifts to make the best for yourself and others, to create the life you want, one you can be proud of.

Be careful of rigid language and thinking. That said, you should always be kind, and never be cruel. Have principles, but be tolerant. Know that passivity, assertiveness, and aggression are not the same things, and being emotional is not a weakness. Being emotional allows for empathy, and empathy is an integral part of compassion and understanding. Try not to please others at the sake of yourself but make sure to remember that everyone is walking a hard road. Be as sensitive and caring to tragedy as you are to joy. Do not be hateful. There already is too much hate on this planet. We need more gardeners sowing gentleness, patience, beauty, understanding, graciousness, and love. Have passion. Be grateful. See the world. Go where you feel energy. Let your passion give you wings and let your love give you roots.

Understand that decay is a sad but inevitable part of life. All things supple will wrinkle, rot, fade, and die. You will be hurt. You will be hurtful. Be merciful and forgive others their frailty and bad behavior, even when it causes you suffering. That is the only way for you to be free. I will provide you with safety and warmth, the constancy of my abiding love, but my protection and good intentions cannot prevent you from knowing pain, or from causing it. I wish it could and yet without misery we would never know true joy. If the tides did not violently batter the shore there would be no tidal pools, iridescent aquatic communities that congregate in the eroded hollows of ancient rock. We are ravenous on this planet, rapacious, we feed on one another cyclically and without mercy, and yet there is food for all. Every one of us is recycled eventually. There is a certain harmony to that.

What you must not miss out on is adventure. It is a journey to come forth, to be born, to quest for meaning and answers and love and breath, of lung, and breadth of experience. There is magic here. It hides in webbed corners guarded by spiders, fireflies gather it at dusk in July, twirling dandelion seeds heavy with wishes know it, as do lovers lost in rainy kisses. The first time you see a rainbow stretch its arms wide, haloing with spectral glory a body of water, earth, or sky, you will see why life is a gift not to be ignored, returned, or discarded. You will love and be loved, not only by me, but hopefully you will know also what it feels like to blend fully with another being, so completely that you cannot distinguish between their skin and your own, so wholly that your souls feel bonded. Relish these moments. Wait for them. Do not rush. There is a season for childhood, it is blissful but brief, and there is a season for adulthood. Trust me and stay a child for as long as you can.

Slowly you will learn why you were called here, what specific talents you possess that make you unique from everyone else.

Take your time discovering what these are, harness and master your powers, with patience and reverence. I cannot guarantee you a long life but if your priorities are right, if you say what you mean, and do what you say, if you live an honest life moment to moment, and stay as present as possible, if you are kind and good and curious and aware and playful, then the role you will play in your life will be starring, and always will others feel loved in your presence.

That is my hope for you, Sweet Child. That you will of course be happy and healthy, but that mostly you will be love. Receive it, give it, embody it. It is with love I call out to you, it is in love that life becomes divine, and only with love can we heal and be healed, whether we are given one second alive or one hundred years.

Always Love,

Your Mother

Welcome

I welcome
the parts of you,

homeless
and afraid,

that have only
known rejection,

and have never
known peace.

Duality

When the masks wear off, who are we. Are we faded,
like the dusty skin of a long since abandoned chrysalis.

Or is it our nature to be divided. From that original
splitting cell, the mitosis of our conception.

If it is, how can we ever really choose from our duality.
Precious good and wayward evil, this and that, me and you.

The crisp winter moon is as deserving as the fecund rays of
summer sun. And when faced truly with myself, there are no parts
I dare abandon.

Poems

I mostly write
poems about
memories
and wishes,
and love
that echoes
far beyond
my bones.
I am like a night
dressed with stars
that does not
end at dawn.
I go on wide
as I am deep,
building these pages
with words enough
that maybe one day
I will be able
to finally reach
all I desire.

February Afternoon

I don't have the answers
to so many questions
you already are asking.
I can't promise you
an even tide to sail on,
or skies without storms.
I will never be more
than one woman,
who sometimes fails,
while trying her best.
You will be scared.
Your heart will ache.
How I wish that weren't so.
And yet, as I lie here on sunny sheets,
while you play with dinosaurs,
excited when you finish a game,
my heart fills with a love it feels
has the power to carry you.
I admire your profile,
the gentle curves
of your lips and nose,
the way your proud smile
looks at me for praise,
you eager to share your wins,
and inside the balmy folds
of this February afternoon,
I wonder if maybe, for you, my son,
everything will be okay.

Rain in the Trees

There was rain
in the trees,

it felt fresh
and sweet,

like the moment
after
an exhale
before the body
remembers to

breathe in.

We waded through
woods,
unfound on any map,

and I felt
native
to my skin,

and free.

Motion

I am drawn to motion because it is filled with energy. There is nothing static or stagnant about the ocean, or flowers elegantly adorning a windblown perch. Motion inspires emotion and energy connects us with the Universe.

The prairie, the wind, birds, my mother, grandfather, son, and his biological father, all enthusiastic, lively, and kinetic. Full as the deepest ocean, or strongest wind, with life force. Even the trees I best like - weeping willows, and Southern oaks draped wildly with Spanish moss - are active, engaged fluidly in a perpetual dance with life.

I can be more passive. Not always. I skate and dance, sing and write, I love experiencing the diversity of this planet, with food and travel, by playing the piano, or ukelele, by participating in sacred and more casual daily encounters and conversations, but I also am introverted, sometimes reclusively so, and I can get stuck, even paralyzed.

When I see a pink sea rose charge itself against the light of the sun, when the ocean tumbles forward and recedes, it is like I am able to, for a moment, not be then or there, but now and here.

Motion is present and that is its gift, allowing emotion to dominate over thought, or at least join with it, like two partners, in the most organic of dances.

Level to the Gods

Level to the Gods,
those of mountaintops,
like Olympus,
we walked.

Slender, crooked roads
perched above the sea
rose past old doorways
into groves plump
with lemons.

Ancient,
those five towns
of earth, wind,
sun and salty air,

but no more so
than our love,
forged by her womb,
and bonded
by the heavens.

Sweet As Honey

Spires of rock rose
like stalagmites,
punctuating
the horizon.

Atop each
solitary peak
holy structures
stood vigil,

guardians
unchecked
by time.

We dined on beets
and garden potatoes
sweet as honey

and conversation
so rich
I can still
taste the memory.

The land of my heart
is slow and warm
lizards lie lazily
in sun puddles
pelicans park
on old wooden posts
wild horses
are prairie seneschals
and flowers bloom
without season
in antique towns
garnished
with Spanish moss
people say "please"
and "thank you"
and never
is a night
too dark for clouds
this land sings
with tree frogs
with drawls
unhurried
that welcome you in
for tea
sweet and cool
sings with springs
that glisten
with children
and the soft
melody of home.

Greater Than My Understanding

A free thinker I am not.
I like that my eyes
are wet with stardust,
that scattered
in the cells of my bones
are generations of dreams,
that nowhere
in the landscape of my soul
is a flower
that was not once a seed.
The soil
that collects my footsteps
is old, I like it that way,
solid as the oak,
and tiers of rock
that hedge off a tumbling sea.

Give me poetry,
music,
a luscious kiss,
the wings of the raven,
the sigh of the wind,
and I freely cede
my mortal will
to a force
greater
than my understanding.

My Wish Come True

You were my wish.
To be your mother
into the ether
I called
and between
there and here
you agreed to
in this space
that makes a life
with me
be home.

Below the Still Line

The moon was blue
and oleander bloomed
at the crest
of ancient caves
cradled by the sea

I sunk below
the still line
dividing worlds
into the watery womb
where life began

I ceased for once
to be me and I
became instead
a drop in the pool
of eternity

The In Between

we are born and guaranteed
only that death will come
the in between is ours
to fill with meaning
and subtract with moments
do we wisely write our stories
or is the authorial pen
not ours truly to hold
what hallowed truths remain
when from our hollowed walls we go
it hurts to be alive
to never know each day
what is coming
only what has been
that good or bad is gone
unwanted some who touch us
while others we welcome in
we are the sum of each experience
the cells of time
combine without distinction
the illusion that anything divides us
starts wars and ends marriages
we come from the same primordial place
and there we will return
it has no name
yet gave us ours

My Wild Heart Desires

my wild heart desires
to not be haunted
I want the filament of
every fantasy fulfilled
to like the flower
let the bee alight
on petals lush with pollen
that I give without taking
I want not to waste my youth
on worry or fear
to lick the spoon
of a bowl full of batter
I want wind and water
a steady hearth
a passport full of stamps
I want to be heard and seen
and loved for who I am
not who I could be
I want to be read to
beside an old tree
to see my son grow up
I want a musical life
and more time with my parents
hot sand between my toes
someone to dance with
to once have a man I love
look at me with pride
days that last longer than nights
I want peach juice on my chin
kisses that erase thoughts
no more poison or cruelty
I want to give birth
cook with butter
take hot baths
to feel sunlight and beautiful
to make love not hate
with life and myself

to feel content
and confident in my choices
I want passion
but not without kindness
and a legacy of love

This Time

I fall
in love
this time
with myself

I Believe

I believe in dreams
the kind that grow old and wrinkle
that wake us up
with sounds soft and eager
like the wordless breaths
of a child meeting the sun
I believe in belief
in not saying no
to that internal eternal yes
in standing with someone
for something not found on a map
but that still has a key
that beats like the heart
that dreamed us all into existence.

Things I Love

lavender
the juice from a freshly peeled orange
an unhurried hug
the way the light lingers in the gloaming
a really good slice of pizza
being caught in a rainstorm
fireflies
a cold glass of water
the way my son laughs
loose fuzzy socks
the shape of words
connecting with people who get me
music
my mother's coconut brown eyes
pajama days
eating my favorite foods first
waterparks
sleeping well
passion that leaves no space for doubt
poetry
a galaxy full of stars
piano keys
the childlike freedom I feel skating
people who see with the heart
rainbows
how my dad holds my son
people and things with history
relationships that last
onion grass
weeping willows
popovers with strawberry butter
a handwritten letter
photographs
fields full of flowers
how gardenias smell like songs
people who know how to cry
soft fabrics

the voices and faces of my loved ones
a really good story
beach days
wild things
typewriters and vinyl records
art fairs
travel
intelligence
soul

Brushing Into Time

We are like clouds
gathered by the wind,
ephemeral wisps
brushing into time.
So briefly we are here.
We appear and vanish,
into the soft surrender
of an eternal sky,
with only a few
to witness us.
Our shapes are held
by those watchful hearts,
the hearts that beat
deep into the
space beyond this
temporary life,
past tomorrow
and into infinity.
Love holds on
when everything
else lets go.
And for that reason,
no beginning
will ever have
a true end.

What If?

What if tomorrow never comes?
Would today be enough?

Everything and Nothing

lovingbitchyprudeinnocentslutsurvivorvictim
princessloserrebeldorkcaretakerdramaqueen
troubledbossybrilliantcreativeoutsidermean
wonderfulvibrantsexypopularfairymisfitkind
beautifulweirdnaiveautisticspoiledstrong
clingyinsecuresweetgoddessamessgenuinetrue
loyaloutcastoddempathmoodysillystupidreal. . .

I rather see myself as the
volcano breathing under an ocean of water
the single stem that reaches for the sun
the waves of windswept willow leaves
the air between two leaning lips
I have horns and a halo
I am everything and nothing
and always I can be better

emotionalcheaterconfidentgirlywomanmother
daughtersisterfriendgranddaughterauthentic
dreamerunrealisticirresponsiblesophisticated
culturedcruelabusedabusivefoolishromantic
homebodynomadhippiegypsybohemiantraveled
curiouscoldwelcominghomemakerwriterwild
annoyingangryevolvedwisefoolishunique. . .

On the Other Side of You

I know only this skin I am in
on the other side of you is always me
and daily do I struggle
to in this knowledge be loving and free
I have gold in one green eye
my smile is made with heart
my life I would give for my child
and every part of me is art
the words that dance to songs
composed lovingly by my soul
the colors I hang on my walls
how I lift a spoon to mix a bowl
I am a small but mighty woman
and also I am a girl
I am my failures and my flaws
in summer flowers I still twirl
I see magic in minutiae
what hurts hurts me by my hand
I believe in hope and family
that life best lived is unplanned
I am not a perfect person
but I rise when I want not to
to myself I should more utter
my rarely offered sacred love you

The Heartbeat of the Earth

there is soul in these places
in the mountains and the trees
in the wind that kisses my eyelashes
in the sun that warms my skin
the wood feels my pain
sturdy as it is in rings it knows
it speaks of ancient times
when love was not
some word to be broken
but a steady pulsing truth
like the heartbeat of the earth

Sinking Into Solitude

I steep in waters unabided
sinking into solitude like oil of lavender
it is quiet in this simpler space
that does not fill with arguments
or empty with expectations
there is no one to fail to impress
as the moon and sun swap shifts
just a record full of songs
and my baby here to dance with

Medicine

this pen drips doses
of the medicine
my heart needs to heal

Beauty Is Everywhere

I love our planet.
Not because it is always or even often nice
but because elephants exist
and sanctuaries for them to be free
as do people who care and cultivate the land
and make things by hand
and there is all this love,
truly a surplus,
eager for a home.
I ask and go and see and try
and I am better for the experiences,
whether they be emotional,
cultural,
spiritual,
intellectual,
or physical.
Even the pain,
as long as we survive it,
serves a learning or artistic purpose.
Beauty is everywhere.
And innocence.
No matter what else awful there is.

Anchor in Infinity

a series of nights for you I was
no more or less than hundreds
but for me who had in torpor
tread with tepid feet from trauma
you were the bated exhale
an anchor in infinity
the one I awaited without knowing
the arms that made me a woman
could now I let you go I would
no history entwines us
but this famine feasts on memories
and how it felt finally to heal

Follow Faith

I follow faith
because stars
are in the eyes
of children
and faithful
are the fairy tales
of my fantasies

The Only You

do you ever just want to meet someone
on a train passing a field of sunflowers
someone with a scar across their eyelid
someone holding a cup of coffee in a crowded shop
say to them without worry or agenda
I see you, yes, your chambord scarf
or the way you crack your knuckles
but also who you are when the lights
go down in a starless sky
or when you have lost your favorite person
say to them you are not alone
here in this world of a billion faces
say to them happy or sad it is okay
because you are the only you
this world will ever see
and you are beautiful

Meant to Be Yours
(a Halloween Spell)

when the moon is left of the farthest star
and the willow weeps her last tear
bathe your fears in wild lavender
add thyme and dust with passion
paint into your skin slow dripping molasses
and into the beckoning arms of death
scream "not yet" as you dance
naked in magnolia perfumed alabaster light
for what truly is meant to be yours

The Seed to My Blossom

on ancient rocks in wild seas
in childhood I dreamed
of oscar, grammy, tony
my name in lights
and bound on books
the dress I would wear
walking toward my future
but having you inside me
the seed to my blossom
I felt warm and at home
at last in my skin
you reminded me
that on the other side
of darkness is always light

In This Moment

in this moment
everyone remaining is alive
the people who want to be in my life are
I have food and water and shelter
there is no immediate physical danger
my baby looks at me like he won the lottery
I am lucky to have so much

The Price

even if we could
the clock rewind
the price would be
this present

Mine Alone

this soft light now
that surrounds me
has no shadow
it takes no sacrifices
it is mine alone

A Simple Morning Routine

it is a simple morning routine
I open your bedroom shade
play the musical jellyfish
you smile arms raised
in your fuzzy blanket sleeper
for me to hold you and I do
we rock in a white chair
while you have breakfast
I nuzzle and kiss your forehead
tell you "I love you"
you smile with rainbow eyes
as you point to pictures, my nose
what sweet, soft sounds you make
and today sixteen wild turkeys
pranced through cinnamon leaves
a parade across our front yard
a squirrel ate pumpkin from our patch
inside we danced to Amalia Rodrigues
spinning on the Dual record player
my father gave me for Christmas
and we listened to dragon tales
with an audience of plush animals
it is in the moments we stop searching
we find what we are looking for

Wintery Tastes

lands crest with white
a water crystal dream
that twinkles like frosting in the moonlight
sugar sprinkles on trees and cookies
and with lights hangs peppermint
my cocoa cup melts marshmallow
hot in my cold hands
the embers from my fire
flavor the air with smoky wood
into cozy hollows creatures tuck
for months bursting with nutmeg and gifts
like the sound of your laughter
and the taste of new beginnings

True Power

true power does not contend
with loud and striking voice
or a thunder of skin
for control or territory
it takes a giant to be small
willingly and soft
to not seize but cease
to stall the assault
to be new again even after
pain is all that is remembered

See Me Beautiful

see me for my ugly
and call me beautiful

The Not Getting

maybe it is the not getting
that gives us the most
after all you are not his
you were born of another love
had my wish been granted
had he not left how he did
the single worst event of my life
would not have let in the best

What It Felt Like to Believe

in this world glitter frosts houses
lighting up dark streets
and children come in all ages
no wish is too big for a miracle
and worries get the day off
presents come with bows
but also presence
where people near and far
gather around trees born to shine
for a short while songs fill the sky
cheering dashing reindeer
and babes show us how to be
full of love and hope they cry out
in mangers and in firelit rooms
for us to remember
what it felt
like to believe

The People I Like

I like the broken ones
the artists
people who feel
people who cry
people with passion
and something to say
people who stick around
and share of themselves
their hearts and souls
and minds full of stories
the misfits with scars
who never get chosen
the romantics
and the old-fashioned
people with honor and respect
who fight for something
anything with meaning
who know life is brief
but precious and beautiful
the intimate people
who are sturdy and smart
deep and patient
people who are sensual
who are afraid
but do it anyway
people who want a dialog
and are into family
people who hug well
and have substance
and are messy
who mean their moments
but are not mean
people who like adventures
and having fun
who celebrate holidays
and the average Thursday
people who give toasts and thanks

who are into movement and music
who can dance
regardless of how they look
people who breathe in and out
every day that it hurts
even when they would rather stop
the truth tellers and nature lovers
who create of life
and are loving
I like these people
all of them
people like you
and people like me

Like the Birds

my sky splits blue
as I becòme more
like the birds
whose inner compass
guides them home

Roots and Petals

without these roots
that hold me
I am petals
in the wind

The Melody of My Beating Heart

dried marsh grass the color of burnt oat
rests beneath a burnished aluminum sky
as a dancing pine bends to the will of the wind

in a pool by a sea that wanders through reeds
like a snake without specific destination
water collects the way wading birds hungry for river fish do

is the heron wrong for wanting nourishment
are my atoms that seek to fuse with yours
are we messengers or messages of this great land
that carves days out of seasons spanning years

I think what I will leave behind and how the clock will tick
while all I ever have to hold is this crystalline moment
wrapped in the melody of my beating heart

Just Because

just because
it has not
happened yet
does not mean
it never will

Past

the past has no future

Things That Do Not Hurt

an ache awoke me this morning
from the belly of my dreams
I rose, trying to remember
things that do not hurt, like
rainbows that halo the sun
a really good game of Scrabble
a necklace made of flowers
my mother's homemade meals
the hugs my son now gives me
the smell of fresh crushed herbs
l'hirondelle by burgmüller
and anything played on ivories
the clatter of seashells
petrichor and calming blue
the quality of a lasting kiss
these all with me I take
and gradually I feel better

The Faint Echo of Mermaids

golden light fills
pockets of sand
where footsteps have been
while a sisterhood
of birds sing songs
of protection
over their young
how fleeting every roll
of the fickle tide
that covers horseshoe crabs
and mounds of seaweed
and yet this place
with its halcyon gloaming
is so tenderly
embedded in my heart
I feel as if
I must be made
of the same salt
that purses my lips
and the faint
echo of mermaids

Stardust Shadows

I am made of
rainbows,
shadows,
and stardust.

Forever You Are Loved

what if now were it
the end to the story
who with you
would you want there
to share goodbye
do they know their value
that without them
this planet is just a rock
in a vast and hollow space
do they know they are
the home that has no walls
but always has the light on
do they know one blink
will not erase them from view
we live when things
are built to break
and the living become ghosts
we never know when time
will swallow us whole
so to the people
who are the journey
and the destination
your souls shape my heart
and forever you are loved

Open Door

my open door
waits for you
to walk through

Until You Believe

repeat
until
you
believe
this

I am loved

Where I Am My Focus

I woke up this morning
and you were not for once
the first thing on my mind
I visited with my books
I heard the crow who every day
tries to by me be noticed
and when I saw your face
those eyes I for years believed
were the color of the soil
that would grow my future
I did not feel the same way
you were a beautiful fantasy
I needed to save my life
I have never felt more present
or certain and alive
but the reality I see today is
you do not love yourself enough
to honestly love others
so anyone who has you
will only ever have pieces
I need more than a mirage
I need someone who shows up
when a child is born
and does not block love
as a way to practice life
and with or without you
whoever you may truly be
I need more mornings like this
where I am my focus

The Pages of My Story

it was in solitude
that I read
the pages of my story
with my heart

Free

I am becoming
like the wild things –
free

The Liminal Space

I am building a life
in the liminal space,
a foreigner to this time.
My candescent heart
fires new pathways
through the dark.

Gently Discover

I have needed this time.
To rest and pause.
To not rush,
from one sacrifice
to another.
To gently discover
who I am now.

Your Kind of Weird

choose the people
who make you laugh
more than cry,
who make Wednesday
feel like the weekend,
who you can talk with
about the old days
as you make new memories,
who do not need you
to be better or different,
who are your kind of weird
and their kind of beautiful.

Me

And still,
with all my broken pieces,
the things I cannot do,
or understand,
the parts that are less beautiful
and more damaged,
even if some dreams
never come true,
I would rather be me
than anyone else.

In One Face

We are beautiful because
in one face is every face,
all our parents and grandparents,
sisters and brothers.
Our smiles are made
with generations of love,
our ancestry is hope
for a lovelier tomorrow.
And in that way,
we are never really alone.

Flowers

Flowers remind us
there is magic
in this world.

Soul Remedies

It is amazing,
what a little sleep,
and some sunshine,
can do for the soul.

We Make Art

We make art together,
mother and child,
a heart, a star,
a wave of connecting dots.
A crow welcomes dusk,
much brighter these days,
and you draw with two pens,
a new picture of night.
Much less lonely,
and filled,
with the eternal promise
of tomorrow.

Heroes

So many heroes
pass through
the walls of time,
that look
something like you,
and also like me.

To Love

My soul.
My mind.
My heart.
My body.
In that order.

In Balance

Find more ways to laugh.
Seek out something silly.
Not to hide what hurts,
but to keep yourself in balance.

Waving to the Trees

Can all moments be like this,
barefoot beneath a sky of leaves,
you with two fists full of earth,
and us waving to the trees?

The Breath Between Words

perhaps balance
never fully exists
except for in
the breath between words,
in the blink
between glances.

I have long been fascinated by the extremes within human nature, and the external nature of things, but being balanced, and thinking about it, are vastly different. And yet, between words, between glances, between thought and action, feeling and creation, between the two sides of every coin, is the center point, or space, that is occupied by nothing and everything simultaneously.

The balance.

When life brands us as bad, and we believe it, or we promote our good, while shunning our shadow sides, we are not in balance. We are forever tilted, and unsteady. And the people around us can't know or love us fully, nor can we ourselves, because we are either day without night, or night without day, and in being only one, we become kind of neither.

The shore flattens because of the rise and fall of waves, and we are made by everything good and bad about ourselves, and others. It is my nature to want things clear, kind of obvious, and constant, but I also want healing, of which I believe balance is a core part.

If balance is the space between, maybe I have to embrace a more fluid set of expectations, and daily practices, starting with myself, and what is honest for me when I am less tilted, and more evenly bad and good. Because I definitely have, and need, both.

My Power

and the very things
that most have threatened me,
are how I have gained my power.

Who Make Your Soul Smile

Keep in your heart,
the people who
make your soul smile,
and let everybody else go.

Giant Heart

your tiny frame
holds inside
a giant heart
that believes in love
and echoes eternity

More Careful Consideration

and if, what feels right to me,
feels wrong to you,
does it not, therefore, deserve
more careful consideration?

Released

trauma trapped my voice,
in a cage with no oxygen,
until this ink released me

Someone

never be someone
who becomes
someone else
for someone

On Our Own

learning
who we are
on our own
improves
all of our
relationships

As You Are

Nobody
could ever be
as beautiful
a version
of you
as you are.

Losing Race

we cannot
outrun
who we are

Old Friend

Sometimes, all we need
to feel home again,
is a little time,
with an old friend.

Legacy

Not everyone we love
is going to love us back.
Do not become bitter,
hardened, or mean,
do not numb yourself
to the sun as it rises
every lucky day we get here,
or forget why only you
will be beautiful
just as you are.
It is our dreams come true,
but also our disappointments,
that shape our destinies,
so be gentle with yourself
as you heal whatever hurts,
take your time and stay kind.
This life will be over soon enough,
and your legacy,
will be how you are now.

Heart Creation

Let your life
be the creation
of your heart.

I, Alone

I, alone, know
the steps it took
to arrive at this
moment in time,
what mountains
I crossed and
storms I beared,
on this long
and tangled road,
that threads through
the days of my life.
This path I clear
does not belong to me,
but it is mine still,
and I choose
to keep walking.

Proud of My Heart

I am proud of my heart.
It has been through a lot,
but it stays loving.

Whatever It Is

It could be as simple
as having a bowl of oats,
or sinking into a tub
bubbling with lavender,
but whatever it is that
restores and recenters us
is what we need more of,
and we need to let go
of whatever takes us farther
from who we are inside.

All I Have

I may not have the guy, but
I have friends, and flowers,
and family who love me, I have
the wind, right before it rains,
and clouds, that in the summer sky
take on mythological shapes, I have
taste buds that give me pumpkin,
onion, and peach melba, I have
dancing feet, a beating heart,
Pete Fountain on the stereo
that plays while I am making meals,
I have conversation, and thought,
I have song while I drive, and dreams
while I sleep, and passion fills my
every cell. I may not have the guy,
and that does make me feel sad,
but what I do have is quite a lot.

Unconditional

Love does not
bargain for
conditions.

On the Street Where I Live

on the street where I live,
the old man walks his dog,
kids splash in a wide pool,
trees wave to their ancestors,
bushes of black raspberries grow wild,
and I sit here, tending our days,
with the love of a mother
who wanted her child more than
any other dream that could ever be,
he puts stickers on his crib,
he dances freely to every beat,
he gives my heart its home,
and I could see this as forever,
me by a rose of sharon tree,
with him showing me the way.

Celebrate You

may today be the day
you decide to forever celebrate
the amazing person you are.

In My Seasons

the flowers know
when they are ready,
and the trees,
browning slightly
as they give way to fall,
blossoming proudly
with the first kiss of spring,
so why is it so hard for me,
to be in my seasons,
to say yes to the life
I have waiting for me now,
to not run from tomorrow

Be You

Be sad. Be scared.
Be scarred and hurt
and utterly confused.
Be breaking. Be lost.
Be so completely stuck
you cannot move at all.
But be here. Be you.
Be where you actually are.
Be present for yourself,
with whatever you
are going through,
for as long as it
decides to take.
There is no rush.
This is your story.
And you deserve
to be here.

Something New

Sometimes,
we need someone new,
to feel something new.

Someone Who Knows

I need someone
who knows who they are
and what they want,
who pursues me,
and knows what passion is,
who never lets me question,
when I go to sleep at night,
or wake up every morning,
that to them I matter,
someone who kisses me
like I am the air they have
been waiting to breathe

A Happy Middle

Everybody always talks
about a happy ending,
but endings are never happy,
I would rather have
a happy middle.

What We Want

The people we
pretend to be
will never get us
what we want.

I may be intense,
but I like that about myself.
I am not a faint-hearted lover.
I take people all the way in,
into my fears and my focus.
I am the ocean, deep and wild,
breaching waves, like all it has
ever wanted to do is dance.
I am not a shallow pool,
shrinking into dry grass.
I am the rain that raises flowers,
and the sun on the back
of a butterfly's wings.
I am fire. I am wind. I am earth.
I am questions and their answers.
I am from and of the storm.
I shed emotion with that kind of fury.
Indifference will never waste me away.
My trunk is wide, my roots are long,
my pledge understands forever.
It is the look a mother gives her baby,
the moment after he has been born,
and it is the infinite spiral of a universe,
that even inside the vacuum
of a collapsed and languid space,
remembers how it felt to love.

West of Yesterday

The sun set
west of yesterday,
and I sat
on two planks of wood,
marsh grasses dancing
with the warm evening wind,
wondering if you
will ever sit here with me.

See With Heart

If we saw with our hearts,
and not our eyes,
would we treat others better?

Add or Subtract

The most important question
for any dating single parent,
"Will this person add or subtract
happiness, in my child's life?"

So Good

I could be bad with you,
and that felt so good.

When Life Was New

Who were you
when life was new,
before you learned
anything could be
wrong with you?

A Whiskey Love Song

The sea was foggy,
our conversation
compass for a moon
that watched over us
without showing its face.
It had been years
since I had seen eyes
hunger for me.
You kissed me,
like you meant it,
as Chris Stapleton sung
a whiskey love song,
where earlier we played chess,
and I remembered how
it feels to be a woman.

In Gold

This I write in gold,
that I will never again
shrink myself down
to a lesser version of myself,
to win the love of another.

Change of Scenery

A change
of scenery
can change
how we see things

Sheltered

Lovers come and go.
Build a nest of people,
family and friends,
who will keep you warm
on cold nights,
and sheltered,
when you need a home.

Meant to Be Free

Do not color me
inside the lines,
or cage me in a box
you tuck into your attic,
for I am meant to be free,
love me that way, or not at all.

Lasting Change

Lasting change happens gradually,
and so much of life is about perspective.
Day to day, we may look the same,
it may look like I am still, only,
a bundle of pain and sorrow,
it can even feel that way to me,
but every moment I am healing,
and redefining what life is now
that everything is different.
My heart aches for what I lost,
but at least I am here to feel,
when there were days not long ago
my existence was in question.
Healing takes time because
it effects every cell, it must
touch every memory with loving hand.
My shattered nose healed faster,
after bullies pushed me down
a concrete flight of stairs,
because it is just one nose.
The heart is all that ever was,
every person, breath, and beat.
Her landscape may look different,
and I know I still get lost,
but I also know how far I have come.
And what I still wish for,
under the starry cloak of night.

The Main Character

Own the story you are in.
Be the main character.
Be proud of how you
are writing your life.

The Song Only You Can Sing
(a Halloween Spell)

When the wind is right
and the moon is high,
with your favorite pen,
write your love a letter.
Add vanilla drops for a loyal heart,
pepper shavings for passion,
yellow rose petals for friendship,
dandelion seeds for magic,
holly sprigs for holiday spirit,
an acorn top for strong roots,
ocean water for emotional depth,
and mistletoe for midnight kisses.
Seal all this together
with the song only you can sing,
and light it with a candle.

Stop

Sometimes, you need to just stop,
slow down, step back, and away,
to still yourself enough inside,
to see what your soul is saying.

Flight and Ash

I took to flight that day,
the day my world fell to ash,
and I have been soaring since.

In Comfort

old friends
wrap our hearts
in comfort

People Who Feel Like Home

Stay close to the people
who feel like home.

Solid

I want words
I can stand on.

See With More

If we only saw
with our eyes,
we wouldn't see
much of anything.

Tapestry of Humanity

People are scared.
People are dying.
Huddled in our homes,
we wonder who is next,
as sickness takes
hold of our earth.
We may be apart
but we are also together,
threaded by our hearts
into one tapestry
of humanity, and love.

The Right Thing

a lot of people will
say the right things.
choose the people
who do the right thing.

Sing

and with
the days
I have left,
let them be full
of everyone,
and everything,
that makes my heart
sing

I Grow a Little More

I am not always kind.
I am not always calm.
I try but often fail.
But I am generous
with my heart,
and open with my emotions,
and every day,
I grow a little more.

Alive Now

We are alive now.
That is all we know, and have.
Tomorrow may never come.
We must be brave,
and embrace life
in all its chaotic splendor.
What we need to say,
what we want to try,
this is the time to do it.

Be Brave

Be brave,
tiny heart,
your time will come.

It matters, what others think,
but I am the only person
who is ever going to be living
in this skin, with these feelings,
and these experiences.
It isn't only me in my story,
but I am the only one who knows
what my life feels like from the inside.
This is why I listen to my heart.
Too often my head has gotten me lost,
stuck in the maze of other people's thoughts,
what they think I should do,
and how they think I should be.
Maybe choosing how I do is wrong,
but, to my heart, there may not be a choice.

Action

Action
illustrates
desire.

It is brave, to speak up, reach out,
to share of ourselves what most hurts
inside the stories we are living,
to not let pain silently claim us,
while we fight our battles alone.
You will never be a burden
to anyone who really matters,
not for one single thing you could share.
We all are battered, bruised,
with paint chipping, and fabric faded,
our sorrows wear all of us down.
But whatever hurts you does not mark you
as any less deserving of love
than anyone else that exists,
and even if some parts of our journeys
are necessarily solitary,
to offer us the most personal growth,
there are people out there who care
about who you actually are,
and who want you to be alive.
And for some, you might be everything,
you, with all your shadows and light,
might for someone be their perfect choice.
Believe in tomorrow, in right now,
but most of all yourself, and all your magic.
It is there. You are real. And so worthy.

My Strong and My Storm

Sometimes I am so scared,
like a little kid too afraid
to ask how to tell time,
and other times I feel mighty,
like an indomitable mountain
cresting an eternal horizon.
I am learning how to
forgive and thank myself for both
my strong, and my storm,
for the times I run and hide,
and the times I stand brave,
despite anything threatening
to break me.

The Gauge

fear can be the gauge
for what is truest
in our hearts

History and Soul

I like things with history,
and a lot of soul.

Rare

I know how rare I am.
Not every heart
is made with poetry,
and the stubborn will
to love with such fire
that nothing can put it out.
I exhale art and passion
pulses through my veins.
I am a masterpiece
of tragedy and triumph,
I am small but not weak,
mortal but still holy,
the phoenix and the ashes,
a star in the blackest night.
I will never break to the point
where hope cannot get in,
life does not have
that crushing power,
I will go on forever,
the brightness of my soul
leading the way.

Through Your Eyes

I love
looking
at myself
through
your eyes.

Maybe

Maybe we get
a hundred years,
to love more,
and hate less,
to take leaps,
and be ourselves,
to make new dreams
out of old ones,
and build relationships
that will last,
to trust in the chances
that present themselves,
and the things and people
that are most real.

Remembering Ourselves

How many of us
learned to believe,
at a young age,
that we needed to be
more of one thing,
and less of another?
They were wrong,
whoever they were.
Who we naturally are,
how we naturally are,
is the exact way
we were meant to be.
As adults, the challenge
is remembering ourselves
before anyone scarred us,
and believing ourselves
worthy of the honest love
we may not always
have received.

The Future Can Be Anything

Things I struggle to remember:
The past is not the present.
Now is not forever.
The future can be anything.

Not Nothing

you will never
leave your side,
and that is
not nothing

To the Beat of an Old Wood Clock

I drink my morning espresso
to the beat of an old wood clock,
that keeps me company
during the early hours.
I think always of you,
people from my past,
who taught me about laughter,
and love so rich
its soil can sprout flowers,
through hard winter earth.
And also the you of my future,
who will take me boldly
into your arms, and heart,
and kiss me in a way
that proves there could
never be a tomorrow
with anyone else.

Intimacy

Intimacy
is the act
of offering
every part
of yourself
to someone
knowing
they may
reject you.

Love Means Something

Maybe nothing lasts.
Maybe most words
are made to be broken.
Maybe we will fade
into forever, mostly unseen.
But love does mean something.
It can be bright, as the moon,
that lights the darkest night,
and as eternal, moving our tides
from one morning to the next,
for the days that make a life.

Every Moment

We are not
who we are
because of only
the things that
have gone right.
The bad things
also make us,
and not just
for the worse.
I am grateful
for every moment
I am given.
The love, loss,
pain, and joy.
The easy wins,
and uphill battles,
all are gifts,
shaping me into
who I am.

Your Goodbye

your goodbye
opened my world
to glorious
new hellos

In Tomorrow

A garden of amber leaves
float down from the trees,
letting go of heavy branches,
so the wind can take them
where they need to be,
now that the seasons have changed,
and we are in tomorrow.

Steadily There

Who shows up for you,
no matter the time
or space between you?
Who is steadily there
with their love?
Cherish the ones
who choose to stay,
who choose you,
in this world of
infinite choices,
because not many will.

Wintry Trail

So many steps we walk
without anyone by our side,
but are we ever really alone?
For at the end of a wintry trail,
where only my feet leave prints,
a nesting mother duck waits with me
as the sun sets fire to the land,
and an ocean that has been here
since the beginning of all that is,
waves hello and goodbye
as if we are old friends.

Only My Heart

I often feel like not enough.
I say the right things
to the wrong people,
or the wrong things
to the right people,
and if I were someone else,
I might have more
of what I think I want,
and less of what I don't.
But this skin I am in
is the home of my heart,
and only my heart
beats this way,
a way that lets me see
things that are invisible,
a way that lets me feel
the poetry of the earth.

Heaven

Maybe heaven
is all the tiny
moments of perfection
our souls bring
from one lifetime
to another.

Side of the Road

Sometimes, the best view,
is on the side of the road
we are travelling on,
and if we don't stop,
and take special notice,
we will miss it.

Rainbow Storm

I am not honestly sure,
if I am more the rainbow,
or the storm.

An Act of Rebellion

These days,
an act of rebellion
may be in wanting
more old-fashioned things,
like a flag waving proudly,
and small town life,
neighbors saying hello,
and how are you doing,
a home to grow some roots,
full of children
and homemade popsicles
and messy art projects,
men who still open doors,
a spouse to grow old with,
holidays together,
and meals cooking on the stove.
Being modern, and progressive,
is letting a woman
be however she wants,
and letting a man do the same.

Fortresses

These fortresses we build,
mostly around our hearts,
do not guarantee safety.
They may keep others out,
but they also shut us in,
shackled to our shadows.
The ways we are set in
serve the past,
more than the present,
and any chance we have
for future happiness.
Taking a leap of faith
may mean that we fall,
not every risk has a reward,
but at the edge of tomorrow,
I would rather be free,
than a prisoner
of my own making.

Pandemic

This pandemic has taken a lot.
People, and the way life was.
But it also has shown us,
more clearly than anything could,
who truly cares and matters,
and how we want our lives to be.

Things That Bring Me Joy

Nature brings me joy, my son, and other loved ones,
sunlight, flowers, music, the sound of the birds,
colorful things, art, good food, crickets, connecting
and provocative conversations, beach days, deep hugs,
a long lavender tub, fresh sheets, how words can
become things (with the right amount of soul), dancing,
reading cookbooks, raw honesty between people (when
the barriers are down), walking outside, listening
to the wind through the trees, garden time, board
games, fireflies, musical theater, movie marathons,
cultural immersion, new ways of looking at old problems,
long walks, my breath, spontaneous adventures, home,
passionate moments, pandas, rain falling on the roof,
newly fallen snow, spring crocuses, home cooking,
sweet tea, rainbows, storm clouds, secret glens,
someone I love contacting me, an easy back and forth,
toasts and reasons to celebrate, a really good question…

Shadows

We are not defined
by the worst of ourselves,
what we have done,
what secrets lurk beneath
the surface, who we are,
without any lights on.
Our shadows do not
brand us as undeserving.

Time Can Tell

I prefer
the stories
only time
can tell.

Eclipse

Into the woven
chrysalis of
new beginnings
my ancient
mortal skin
uncoils
to reveal
the eclipse
of one self
for another.

Circles

I love it
when the wind
blows circles
around my thoughts.

Value

If you did it,
said it,
felt it,
carried it,
than it is real
for you,
and it has
enormous
value.

Temporary People

I don't want to
populate my life
with temporary people.

The Kind of Love

may you have
the kind of love
that always
includes you

Not a Casual Person

I am not a casual person.
I am deep waters,
the ember of an undying flame.
To connect with
the culture of a soul
for me is rare.

Make Space

make space
in your heart
for the people
who stay

Little Rays of Sunshine

compliments
are like little
rays of sunshine
scattered throughout
a life

Open

sometimes a break up
breaks us open
to love even more

This World Needs You Here

maybe there will be a limp,
or a scar, or a place in your heart
that never feels quite right again,
but today is not yesterday,
and you have gotten this far,
and you are stronger than defeat,
stronger than terror, and loss,
and the hopeless persuasion
that you are not enough as you are,
because you absolutely are,
you are everything you need to be,
and this world needs you here

The Biggest Mountain

The biggest mountain
most of us will climb
is our acceptance
and love of ourselves.

Between

I am between.
Between breath and sound.
Between no and yes.
Between breaking and healing,
past and future,
birth and death.
I am the voice
that speaks without words,
somewhere between
my head and my heart,
and between faith and fear,
I also am there.
I am between.
And always becoming.

Fervent Wish

what is faith
but the fervent wish
that the heart
is not a liar

Some Moments

some moments are more
than seconds on a clock.
they take us in, they hold us,
they transform from despair
an unyielding hope, and healing
wider than every yesterday,
that once threatened tomorrow.
some moments bring us
so far into ourselves,
bridging all our fractured pieces,
that we know we will
never be truly lost again.

A Slow Process

Healing is a slow process
that is not linear
and cannot be rushed.
It takes patience,
courage, and gentleness,
more than feels possible,
and sometimes progress
is simply taking another step.

Full of Flowers

some hearts
are full of flowers
because their sun
shines from within

Deep Waters

To get close to me
you have to know
how to swim
in deep waters.

Acceptance

I think true love
is a measure of
how unconditionally
we accept the things
we don't like about someone.

The Gift of Time

and of all
the wonderful gifts
that people give,
the best of them
is time

Soil I Cannot See

The only way
to know whether
the floor beneath
my feet is solid
is to step forward,
but I feel afraid.
I know what is
behind me.
Even the pain,
there, is familiar.
It is like
a too tight shoe,
but that once
walked me all around.
Is there more than air
in tomorrow,
a tree to hold on to
down an unmarked path,
or maybe someone's hand,
can I trust
in soil I cannot see?
What flowers
await me?

Tiny Extra Step

Maybe
it isn't about
reaching some end goal,
about loving ourselves or not,
about doing life the "right" way.

Maybe
it is about
simply loving more.
Loving ourselves more.
Loving each other more.
A little more than yesterday,
a little more than our hurt,
a little more than anger,
than fear, or revenge.

Maybe
it is about
that tiny extra step,
that walks us away from pain,
away from the urge to give up,
away from hate, and sorrow.

The Love You Need

let today be the day
you offer yourself
the love you need

Thunder and Wildflowers

The morning came
like thunder
and wildflowers
and I cried
to be alive
for one more day.

Birdsong

I think if hope
had a sound
it would be
birdsong.

A Little Bit of Art

Happiness is
a little bit of art
on a sad day

Gardens

Land on my petals,
she said to Life.
Take whatever nectar you need.
So that of tomorrow
there will be gardens
where today there is a single flower.

The Season

Perhaps
it is not the dream
but the season
that needs to change

So We Can Fly

sometimes we
have to fall
so we can fly

Important Words

Thank you.
I'm sorry.
Some of the most
important words
that exist.

The Sum

we are the sum
of a history of people
with belief more than doubt,
and love more than fear.

Healthier

If it makes you healthier,
your body,
your heart,
your mind,
your spirit,
then regardless of risk,
it is worth it.

Mosaics

Our broken bits
are like mosaics
the heart glues
into a picture
of personal strength

Fred Astaire Record

Happiness is
dancing
to a Fred Astaire record
while doing the dishes

Alchemy

it takes passion
to make alchemy
of the seconds
on a clock

Your Guide

let the feeling
in your heart,
not the outcome,
be your guide.

Wild Trees

To endeavor to
not merely allow
life to break us,
like branches underfoot
dry from having fallen
during some careless storm.
To penetrate the earth
with the conviction
to take root,
and the courage
to boldly rise,
as wild trees reaching
for an aching sun.
These are not small
or simpering acts,
undeserving of notice.

Not the Light

Sometimes
it is the shadows
we need,
and not the light.

Still Possible

Not yet is not no.
It is still possible
that tomorrow
will be more precious
than yesterday.

Tomorrow Is Today

Tomorrow is today.
The relationships
we tenderly nurture,
and those we let go.
The fears that seed,
and the mountains of faith
that hold us up.
Everything that might be
is embedded in
this ordinary moment.
Power and weakness
are decided now,
by how willing we are
to believe in our
capacity to heal.
So we can be better,
for ourselves
and loved ones,
than we were yesterday.

To Get Comfortable

How long does it take,
to get comfortable enough with a person,
that lies and secrets are unneeded,
and there is no need for walls or arms,
no reason to compete with one another
for justice, status, or territory.
Are we ever absolutely safe to be
as awful or good as we are, to trust
in the permanence of a connection,
to believe that some people will stay,
and we are worthy of that level of devotion.
Do we dare to love without artifice,
with honesty, innocence, and purity,
or will fear rob us of the chance
to know we are good enough as we are.

Clover

Clover may be small
and not so brightly colored,
but her honey is sweet,
and to the bee
she is as beautiful
as the rose.

Brave to Believe

It is brave
to believe
in tomorrow.

The Simple Life

I like the simple life.
Meeting with family,
sinking into a small town
underneath a sapphire sky,
where locals share stories
about the art they have made,
with smiles that could
never be faked, and eyes
that have watched generations
grow from baby to adult.
I like taking things slow,
and making things last,
investing in a moment
that seeds more than a memory,
because by the heart
it has been planted.
I like children laughing
in a field with tall grass,
grandparents becoming
young again, and hearts
that will never grow old.
I like sunlight stacked
by waves pouring into a
horizon that does not end,
and hugs that ask for nothing
but acceptance, and time.

Nourished

let yourself
be nourished,
for life is too short
to starve
body, heart, or soul

Rich

Simple moments,
full of laughter,
and loved ones,
make life rich.

Poised for Change

Be poised for change,
a graceful shifting
of then for now,
inside your heart
that has been waiting,
for maybe it is here
where you regain
your strength and power,
in the company
of people who always
have loved you,
maybe it is time
for you to rise from
all these dusty ashes,
and go forward
into a forever ready
for you as you are.

Movement

movement
has incredible
healing
power

Not at This

In many ways,
as a person,
I fail,
I often feel
like water
that doesn't know
how to freeze
in winter,
but you look at me
in a way that says
not at this

Cracks

maybe,
we are supposed
to break,
so that through
the cracks
our flowers
can grow

The Memory of Autumn

and when life
seems grey
wrap yourself
in the memory
of autumn

In some areas of life, there isn't a whole lot of control. Like with who we love. Or how we feel, at our lowest. There isn't an on and off switch for specific emotions. We can't just transfer our feelings for one person to another, not with any amount of determination, because people are one-of-a-kind and irreplaceable. And sometimes our only choice is to hold on, to whatever we can, for as long as it takes, until things are better.

Like after a major loss. We hold on to loved ones that are around, favorite movies, any meal we have an appetite for, a song that makes us want to dance, and autumn leaves. Time never changes what has happened. Certain events and the corresponding emotions are forever fixed. Nor, in my experience, does time heal us.

However, it does change us, by adding and subtracting things from our lives, which forces within a personal evolution. Like glacial activity on a surrounding landscape, or how the seasons transform the trees.

This morning, as I was looking out at the changing leaves in my yard, such bright and happy colors, filled with sunlight, I thought of how I have gotten through, when everything inside and out seems grey. It is what and who I love, that is what I have held on to. Holidays, family, music, creativity, things that add joy, and brighten life, like the vibrant colors of autumn.

Mercy

I wonder
what peaks
we are kept from
by shame, pride, and fear,
how many relationships are lost
to the need to win,
how many things could be saved
by a little mercy.

Of Time Makes Poetry

I am grateful
for gatherings,
for tender blossoms of love
that withstand
every season, every storm,
and for a heart
that of time
makes poetry.

Fuck Off

It isn't easy
to stare down
the worst fears
we have of ourselves,
and life,
and tell them
to "fuck off."

It isn't easy to
begin again
and again and again…
and again.

But you know what
is even harder?
Giving up on ourselves,
and how far
we have already come.

I have had amazing experiences in my life. Like dining in the Eiffel Tower, and skydiving over Cape Cod. And I dream still, of seeing baobab trees in Africa, or sitting on a beach in the Solomon Islands. But while my son naps, I was thinking of him, of my mother, and my father, of my grandparents, and brother, when we were kids, of my little dog, and my friends, and other family members, of the men I have loved, of college years, and childhood days, and everything since.

No matter what I have left to do, and dream, and be, it is the simple moments, for me, that I will most remember. Like taking the hand of the woman who grew me, or the tiny fingers of the child I grew, as I cuddle up to them on the couch. I will remember smiling with my father at an herb garden, and walking hand in hand with my best friend around the world. I will remember lying safe inside strong arms, next to someone who smelled like the woods, and kissing my son's ears after he was handed to me in the delivery room. I will remember crunching down buttered popcorn from a big shared bowl during movies, and having meals in familiar company.

That is what will be there with me most, when my road ends. It all makes a life. Grand things, like eating mofongo by a rainforest, next to a bioluminescent bay, and more mundane things, like wrapping gifts for Christmas morning. Our lives fill with sorrows and triumphs, strangers and family. But when great walls fade, and houses change, and new trees grow old as I am, it will be moments like these, next to people I love, the passports through time without any stamps, that will truly have made my life a success.

Snow on Christmas Eve

may I always get excited
by the little things,
like a bowl full of apples,
and snow on Christmas Eve

Bridges

never burn a bridge
you may one day
want to cross

Yet to Bloom

try to believe
that still within you
are flowers
yet to bloom

Trying

I am trying,
trying not to see
a melting sun
while admiring snowflakes,

trying to keep
my heart stronger
than crumbling leaves,

trying to believe
that still within me
are flowers
yet to bloom

Why I Am Alone

We can love ourselves
and also see
why we are alone.
My intensity
scares people.
I can be too much.
Too excited, too in,
too honest, too fast.
I don't mean to push,
to be forceful
or demanding,
and something
meant to stay
won't ever leave,
but some days
my body just wants
to feel something good,
and time's gravity
is so heavy
I rush things
that are meant
to go slow.

Heart Candle

Light a candle
in your heart
that never
goes out.

Journey

We journey back
to find lost things,
like eyes to wake up to,
and arms wrapped around
the slope of our back,
perhaps the smile we wore
during gentler times,
when strawberries were picked
from a backyard bush,
and lemonade was sipped
with our grandparents.
These are the moments
we most felt found,
by ourselves, and others,
when little was harsh,
and love was many.
I hold in my heart
what I wish could stay,
not to be stuck,
but like stars
showing me the way home.

Last month I went back to a place I haven't been to in years. I have passed it a few times, on the way elsewhere, but I had never stopped. Twice now I have, stopped. I have gotten out of my car, walked steep steps down to the water, and I have stared at the path that changed my life. I know why now felt like the time. Something left, hopefully not forever, and a part of me was searching for it. Like if I journeyed back, perhaps I would again find what once was there. I saw a prompt about "the journey back" recently and it made me think of the way I am, and why my life sometimes can so be centered in memories.

I think we journey back, not because our present lives are necessarily unpleasant, although of course they can be, but because there are people and things we found in the past that we wish were here with us now. As many elderly people as I ever meet, dear to me they may be, none will ever be my grandparents. And I felt romantic love that was sure. I didn't want to keep looking, because I didn't need to. What was then may be gone but it also guides us. It connects us to who we have been, and who we have known, and why we are here, in this moment in time.

Memories can be like guiding stars when we need them. A place we shared isn't the same alone, but it can help us to understand why we feel the way we do. There was little I had to worry about when my Mom planted strawberries in my childhood backyard, and I ate them straight off the bush, and when I was held by certain arms I felt such cosmic alignment, everything made sense. I guess I feel lost a lot of the time now. Strong, and capable, proud, but also lost. And so I write to clarify for myself, as much as anything, why things are the way they are, with the hopes that these creative words may also globally connect in some way with you, though our specific experiences may differ.

Surrender

I don't know what it feels like
to willingly surrender,
to be at peace with what comes,
and what goes,
especially when a lot of life
is unpleasant.
But we also have little choice
about many of the elements
that make up a life.
We can love a person,
but they have to love us too,
for it to be something
more than a fantasy.
And we can pursue a dream,
but never realize it.
I think growth, and maturity,
come in part from the acceptance
that life is far more about
the middle, than anything else.
Temporal, corporeal, mental,
emotional. Whatever.
And though I have a long way
to go on that journey,
I hope for that kind of balance,
and harmony.

Tentative Steps

tentative steps
still walk
us forward

New Again

snow reminds us
it is possible
to be new
again

Snow

I waded through feet
of glistening snow
as honey embers
of dawn light
brightened
the corners
of morning.
The sky was blue,
and the trees
were tall,
and I was witness
to this symphony
of fresh beginnings.

For Rain

I wonder if a seed, under the earth, remembers what it felt like to blossom, and bear fruit, on the plant where it began. Is that why it pushes above the soil ceiling, into the light of the sun? The memory of rain, inside dry roots?

Is it DNA, or spirit, that more determines our destiny? Some long history of becoming, that passes through generations of flora and fauna, sparked by an exploding star, at the edge of eternity. That is what I see, when I see a flower in a field, I see eternity, what I feel, when I remember a certain pair of eyes, how they echoed love into my bones. We are ancient beings, every one. Forged not by this moment but by all the moments, and lives, leading up to this life. Which is a humbling thought.

This season has been so dry and long, that as I was listening to the rain fall on my roof this morning, I thirsted almost to become it, to stretch past the edge of arid reasoning, into a lush pool of realized desire. I want to not have that be over, to not have the greatest passion in my life be stuck in the past, to become again like a flower on the vine, full of sunlight and water and seeds.

My son remarks with awe and admiration, how great a person I am and job I am doing, as I assemble a Disney LEGO castle, as one example, and I feel proud of who I have become. Someone far stronger than I ever was, and more capable. I am the contrast of weakness and power, of then and now, of longing and actualization. And maybe we all are. Somewhere in the middle. Something in between.

But that doesn't mean I don't wish to be touched again, in a way that brings forgotten parts of me, back to life. That I don't wish, with every part of my being, for rain.

Come Into

come into
the light
that shines
from within you

Integration

what if our good
isn't as good
as we believe,
and our bad
isn't as bad.
what gifts have
both given us,
and what losses
have both caused.
we should ask ourselves
these questions.
we should examine
the truths we have
accepted as fact.
for no light exists
without shadow,
and night needs both
darkness and stars.
we are shades
of gravity, color,
time, and choice.
healing will only come
when we forgive
ourselves our mortal
flaws and frailty,
and when we commit
fully to the humbling
process of integration.

Recently some of you have written me about what advice I have to offer writers. That is a hard question to answer. I was privileged to get a college honors degree in writing, and I have wanted to write since childhood, it called to me, but it wasn't really until my heart so felt overcome with love, and longing, that writing became me.

These are the things I felt I needed to say, so I could go about my day, and not feel strangled. This is the love I have wished to give, formed by lines and curves, my most unpunctuated and unfettered feelings. Grammar and syntax are helpful, writing can be taught, but it also can't.

Ultimately, writing is emotion. It is accessing the most honest parts of ourselves, our pain, passion, and power, our stories, the people we love, and those who have hurt us, and putting it out there. Putting our hearts, as sculpted by the words we write, to be seen, scorned, and/or valued.

Non-fiction writing is about being so raw you are not sure when you finish if anyone will even ever like you, let alone love you, but knowing you also don't have a choice. Heart is the voice our souls use to speak. And what is connection, which is how writers and readers are made, but souls syncing together.

It wasn't easy for me to talk in public growing up. I was painfully shy. I needed the written word like a life raft. Books to read, The Cape Cod Times jumbles I did at the formica table where my grandparents rented during the summer, to feel unjumbled myself, all I have written. Words have been a safe and supportive space for me, always. A place to run to, and sometimes hide, but always be who I most am.

So I feel to be a writer, first, you have to love words. Love their texture, sound, and meaning. But mostly, you have to love yourself enough to risk everything to be seen, and heard. And isn't that really, writer or not, what we all most want anyway?

The Table

The table waited in the far back corner of a crowded antique store, with only a sooty layer of dust dressing it. It was circular, delicate, but strong, a single pedestal table that once had stood proud, as an elm tree, in a wide field of wildflowers, before being cut and carved to serve diners inside an art deco Parisian café.

This was not its first foray into the commercial market. In fact, the table had been bought and sold many times during its life. So many times that by now it was actually a little confused as to how precisely it came to be resting inside this particular Florida barn. It figured, if it were lax to remember, the points on the map must not be as important as the stories sandwiched between them. So, it let the minutiae go, focusing only on the moments in its life when it had been curious, happy, or when something made it think.

Memory was especially important now, as it was lonely in the store. Most of the table's life had been spent in the company of others. Even when birds used to alight on its branches, or the wind played with its leafy tendrils, the table, then a tree, was never alone. And life as a table was exciting. Food sloshed over brimming bowls, liquid seeping through unstained pores of wood, and the table could taste it. A child would place an amuse-bouche canape of wild smoked salmon with beetroot crème on its surface and the table could smell the briny earthy scent. The table could see tiny rainbows reflected from prisms cast down from the center chandelier. When a man whisked a woman unsuspectingly into a shimmy and a dip the table could feel the dance vibrations. And it was thrilling when the theater rush flooded the restaurant, or a movie star dined with her entourage. Existence now consisted of irregular snippets of conversation from treasure hunters. This hardly served as company. The table, for what felt like years, wiled away its hours observing its surroundings.

Many things it recognized. The blue record box set, stuffed with Fred Astaire records, that lay against the crooked shelf of a homemade bookcase against the far wall, that was familiar. Fred was perched next to Sidney Bechet, exhaling black and white melodies into his reedy clarinet, against a backdrop of maroon. In

228

another life, that record had emptied bottles of Armagnac and closed hundreds of early-morning conversations.

It was a favorite of Michel, who owned Le Chat Noir, the café where the table was first introduced to the world. Bechet always inspired Michel to write. Customers filtered out at their own pace, Michel never rushed them, and once they left, Michel would lock the café door to the outside world, pour himself a thimble full of ouzo, a nod to his Thessalian roots, and with a tiparillo and a stack of loose-leaf paper, he furiously scribbled down words, with such energy and determination that the table could feel every stroke, the sensation not unlike how it had felt to be hewn.

Sometimes the table let the sensation serve as a kind of meditation after a long day. But mostly the table wondered if Michel were recording stories the way it did, or if they were his own stories he told. For all the table knew, Michel could have been filling out a ledger, or an order for specialty cordials and other liqueurs. The table preferred to think of him, however, as a great novelist, whose time had yet to come. The table liked this fantasy because it liked Michel. He was the kind of person who deserved good things. He was kind and interesting, he had a moustache that curled upwards, like his ever-present smile, a booming, jolly voice, and sparkling brown eyes. Michel added happiness to a room, and not just with plates of sugared cherries and bowls of coq a vin.

Other things were familiar too. Mason jars and smoky champagne flutes, etched with floral designs. The table remembered those well. Lavender Royales drunk by women in feathery dresses, Sazeracs from men in tweedy newsboys and straw boaters. On nights people forgot coasters, it felt almost as if the table could taste the Juleps from those jars, the lush green of muddled mint, tantalizing as the tap, tap, tap of Astaire's feet across the record player. Oh, how the table had dreamed of its wooden legs spreading apart into dance, just once, to feel the freedom of a movement it had never known.

The worn-out copy of *A Room of One's Own* reminded the table of the little girl with the pigtail braids, who every day after school, before her single mother picked her up just in time for supper, ordered a vanilla bean float. Michel mixed syrups for her, blending hazelnut with almond, for an especially nutty treat. The girl, Margueritte, read everything, from *Anna Karenina* to *A Tale of Two Cities*, but it was Woolf's book that most seemed to appeal to her. That she carried devotedly in a tattered purse, that hung from her scrawny shoulder like a badge. The table imagined this book most spoke to her because she wished herself to have a room just of her own, although the table had only a hunch and no supporting evidence to confirm this theory.

When it tired of cataloging items, the table replayed conversations. The one where the mother and daughter, who for decades shared escargot, salt-crusted fish with haricot verts, and raspberry soufflé, for the first time had a dinner guest – a busty man who smelled of mothballs and liquorice, and nervously dripped sweat onto the table, from a billowing brow. The table did not like this man because after he diagnosed the elderly woman with cancer, the duo never returned to the restaurant. He missed their animated chatter, how easily they had laughed in each other's company, how effortless their interactions were, and that stopped the instant that fatal news was delivered.

He remembered the young actress who used to recite lines to herself in hushed tones, long passages from *A Midsummer Night's Dream* were his favorite. She had a mousy voice and wore flat shoes, and a velvet lime beret. Every time she sat at the table she was alone, but one day a man came over, who traditionally preferred counter service, and he told her he had been admiring her from afar for years. She gulped and was quiet for a long while, as if she swallowed whole all the words she could possibly reply with, until finally she asked him if he would like to join her. He was a tall man, with a long torso, who kind of hovered above the table when he sat, but the table liked them together, and it was especially happy during the conversation where the tall man asked the mousy actress if she would marry him. They were sharing a sugar cage, Michel's Christmas specialty, and inside the sweet architectural confection was a glistening diamond ring, flanked by pink sapphires. Almost as magnificent, to the table, as the chandelier.

The table received its side ding when two men got into a brawl, uncharacteristic of Le Chat Noir. Edmond and Henrik, the table could never forget their names. A girl incited their ire, not one who was there, but one who they both seemed to want nonetheless. Edmond began yelling, about how Henrik had no class and upbringing to offer the lady in question a future of any promise, and Henrik, a big man with a brindled beard and husky voice, lunged for Edmond almost instantly, flinging the table into the studded brass wainscoting it had long admired, the force of the stylistically raised nail heads denting a portion of its wood. The scar was imperceptible, Michel had later said, when assessing the damage, but the table to this day felt insecure about it.

There even had been a woman, Colette, who had gone into labor at the table. She also was a regular, Le Chat Noir had many of those. One second she was dipping her dainty spoon into a parfait of plump berries, the next a puddle was collecting at the table's base. She managed to remain calm until the ambulance came, breathing only slightly heavier than before, but Michel could not contain his emotions. Clapping hands to his face, Michel dropped a bowl of honey mascarpone, for his famous chocolate peach clafouti, and while leaping over the glossy bar, in one dazzling motion, he knocked over three Chanel Lilies – specialty cocktails of the house. Indistinguishable sentences of French and Greek slipped from his mouth, and Michel's usually grounded voice sounded a bit to the table like the song of the redwings, that once congregated within its eaves. Had the table not known the café was Michel's only family, it might have mistaken him for the baby's father. He held Colette's hand, and dabbed her forehead with a dampened napkin, and later the table learned Colette named her daughter, Michelle Marie, in honor of the man who, without asking anything in return, helped to usher her child into the world.

The table missed Michel, Colette, the aroma of flambéed bananas, and poulet basquaise, it longed to hear Sydney Bechet again and not just see him, it felt dirty and forgotten in that abandoned corner of the world. It wondered if this were death, to remember, alone, or if, far worse, it was destined to one day forget all the people, places, and things that had given its life meaning. No one spoke, no music played, and there were days when it doubted whether Le Chat Noir even existed, that field where its life started amongst the flowers, or if in its loneliness, it had made them all up.

It was in this forsaken state when the table met Pandora. She was a doe-like girl, with green eyes and wavy hair, who wore a loose skirt and an off-the-shoulder crimson shirt. She kind of bounced when she walked, the way a girl does, but she was definitely a woman. The table liked her freckles, they were disarming, and her smile. She smiled a lot, not unlike Michel, but it had been ages since the table let itself think of him. The happy memories, locked deep in the belly of time, at some point became too painful.

"Perfect!" she said. She snuck a mid-century dishrag off the wall, and wiped clean the surface of the table, so no longer was it covered in dust. She replaced the rag and returned to the table. With a hand as smooth as silk she stroked the wizened face of the table. It could have been her lover, or mother, how gently she touched it, as if she had been waiting forever to feel its skin.

She pulled up an aluminum vinyl chair, from a nearby work desk, took a paint-chipped candelabra down from a shelf in an adjacent room, and placed a small bowl and spoon on the table. For some time she sat like that. The table knew imagination and Pandora was lost in it. Finally, she checked the price, hanging in faded ink on a tiny paper slip, suspended by a string and yellowed tape. The table did not know what it was worth, and it suddenly became very scared. It knew it could not stay there alone, not any longer, it desperately wanted to be needed. Remembered. Kept.

And then, just like that, it happened. Its whole life the table had been waiting to be addressed, and no one, not even Michel, had ever directly done so. Pandora replaced the items, removed the price tag tenderly, and spoke.

"Hello, Table. I'm Pandora. I'm opening a café and you are to be my centerpiece. I have been waiting my whole life to meet you."

We are snowflakes on the face of eternity.

Made in the USA
Middletown, DE
10 March 2022

62415415R00146